MW01064510

i

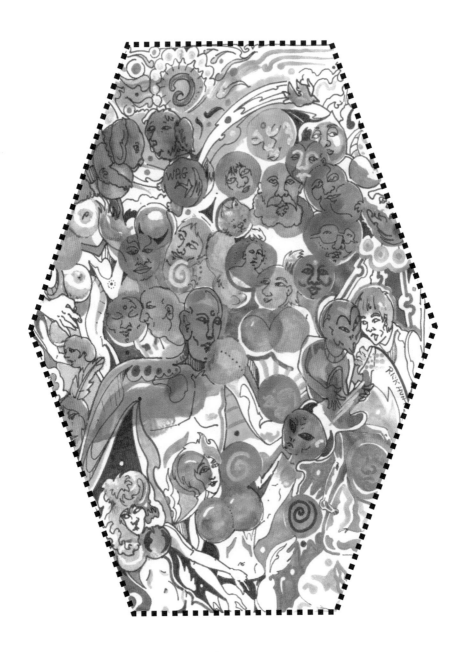

FANCY

FOOTWORK

A POETRY COLLECTION

by

ANGIE BOWIE BARNETT

Illustrations by Rick Hunt

2015

Thanks to the following people for their support in making this book come to life:

Helena Marie Barnett Galas – my mother

Col. George M. Barnett – my father

Stasha Larranna Celeste Lipka – my daughter

Michael F. Gassett – my partner of 21 years.

D.Z.H. Jones – my son

Rick Hunt – my friend and illustrator of this book

Peggy Michik – one of my favorite inspirations and friend

Sergio Kardenas – cover photography

Federico Mastrianni – my friend and photographer extraordinaire

Table of Contents

ANGIE BOWIE

By Adriana Rubio

Author... Actress... Model... Musician... Mother...
Former Wife of David Bowie.

THE EARLY YEARS OF A LEADING LIGHT WOMAN:
Angie Bowie was born on the island of Cyprus in 1949,
the daughter of Colonel GM Barnett and Helena Marie
Galas. Her father was a U.S Army veteran, a mining
engineer and ran a mill for Cyprus Mines Corporation.
Angie grew up feeling like an only child because her
brother was 16 years older.

Angie received her education in Cyprus and at the age
of nine she was sent to St. George's School in
Switzerland. St Georges is an international school for
wealthy people, a place where she felt she did not

belong, but helped her to learn how to survive as an independent-self-sufficient person. "First I had to learn French, then get used to being away from home and having only my own resources to support me. My sense of humor rescued me from extreme alienation, but we were all outsiders at St. George's."

At the age of 16 Angie left Switzerland to attend the Connecticut College For Women in America where she began the journey of her own life. A lesbian relationship with a school mate started and resulted in college interference as was the way with many same sex relationships at that time. "The psychiatrist at the college grabbed my girlfriend and I, and imprisoned us in the surgery. I had to convince a nurse to bring me my clothes, and then I leapt from the second floor window and ran back to my dormitory. I packed and left for Cyprus within a few days."

In 1967 Angie went to England to study at Kingston Polytechnic. Angie Bowie is gifted with a remarkable intellect. She's well read and well informed. England was definitely the place where she felt at home. "I believe the only place I truly felt at home was in England."

In 1968, Angie met David Bowie. He was trying to get signed to Mercury Records. Angie was working with Lou Reizner and Doctor Calvin Mark Lee, both executives for Mercury, so was able to get Mercury to release Bowie's single 'Space Oddity.' Angie and David fell in love, married in 1970 and had a son called Duncan Zowie Heywood Jones. He dropped Zowie when he began his professional life and is now a film director.

THE STARMAKER AND POWER BEHIND DAVID BOWIE:

Angie introduced David to Tony DeFries when he wanted to divest himself of Ken Pitt, his previous manager. Hunky Dory, Ziggy Stardust, Aladdin Sane and Thin White Duke periods are the most productive and ground-breaking years. Angie and David Bowie looked curiously alike and they came together as a terrific package. She has often been referred to as the STARMAKER and the power behind David's meteoric success. The cultural impact of David and Angie Bowie in the 70s led Angie to write 'Free Spirit' and 'Backstage Passes: Life on the Wild Side with David Bowie.' Angie won an award for best audio biography with her audio book of 'Backstage Passes.'

'Backstage Passes' is rumored to be the inspiration behind the film 'Velvet Goldmine.' Angie and David divorced in 1980. And according to what has been said publicly, David Bowie has tried to edit Angie out of his life and deny her contribution to his tremendous success. As a woman, ahead of her time, Angie reacts in a very philosophical manner. "Famous men frequently do that when they feel threatened by a woman's influence. They like to be thought of as the sole instigator of creativity or genius. God forbid that any woman helped them to get where they did. Picasso did the same thing to the woman around him."

David Bowie's songs 'The Prettiest Star' and 'Golden Years' are definitely about Angie. It is openly proven with her appearance in a backstage sequence from the D.A. Pennebaker concert film Ziggy Stardust and the Spiders from Mars where David Bowie calls her by the name "Star." During the 1970s, Angie Bowie accompanied her husband on the majority of his international concert tours and promoted him on radio and television as a celebrity guest on Johnny Carson's

The Tonight Show, in 1973 Russel Harty Show UK and also performed on The Mike Douglas Show in 1975. After which, David wrote 'Golden Years' to acknowledge her performance and singing 'I've Got A Crush on You,' to Mike Douglas as her first public singing engagement.

ACTING TALENT AND FILM WORK:

Angie Bowie is also known for her acting talent. She performed at the Lausanne exhibition in 1964 playing Barberine in the Alfred de Musset play 'Barberine.' She acted all through school and college in the Changeling, Jeanne D'Arc by Jean Anouilh and rejoined and auditioned for the leading role of the telefilm Wonder Woman which aired on March 12, 1974. As Linda Carter already had the role and the auditions were just to satisfy the acting unions, Angie approached Stan Lee in Hollywood and in late 1975, Angie Bowie bought the television rights for the Marvel Comics' characters: Black Widow and Daredevil for developing and selling purposes featuring the two heroes. Terry O'Neill photographed Angie and Benny Carruthers, American actor ('Shadows') and screenplay writer as the characters. Angie Bowie's film work includes acting roles in 'Eat the Rich', 'Demented' and 'The Slayer Bureaucrat.' She took to the stage in Tucson with City Players to star as Alice in 'Tiny Alice', Edward Albee's play.

MUSIC WORK OF A GODDESS:

As a musician, Angie's musical compositions are available on the album CD 'Moon Goddess, and a CD maxi single, 'The World Is Changing' where Angie receives full credit as composer of the lyrics and Morgan Lekcirt wrote and produced the musical track. Various re-mix masters including David Padilla, Tom Reich, Jim Durban and D.J. Trance contributed versions of the song. The musical work was published by Cheetah Records in 1996 on the New York label Warlock Records. 'Moon Goddess' is the CD of her songs and spoken word. 'Obsession' for Paul Zone, she covered the Ramones' tune for Bossa n Ramones and 'The Last Time' is a Stones cover with Jude Rawlins.

PROJECTS, WRITING AND MORE:
In 1980, Angie had her second child, daughter Stacia, with the punk musician Drew Blood. She settled in America concentrated mainly on Stacia's education, but she has also been involved in a number of projects. Angie ran her own horse ranch, was a celebrity editor for the notorious Larry Flynt and has succeeded in her chosen profession of writer. She published, 'Bisexuality: A Pocket Guide', 'Free Spirit', ' Backstage Passes', ' Lipstick Legends' ,' POP.SEX', 'Cat'Astrophe' and now 'Fancy Footwork.'

Angie Bowie lives with her NON-musician partner. Her first solo album "Moon Goddess" was released in 2000. 'Fancy Footwork' is her second album to be released in 2015. Angie is the leading light for women's rights, alternative lifestyles and human equality of the present age!

Rick Hunt

BORN 1955, in Littleton, New Hampshire, Rick studied with internationally known artist, Kenneth Westhaver, privately, and at Franconia College as a teen before attending Massachusetts College of Art in the early 1980's.

RICK'S ART has been shown in such places as galleries and museums and has been published in books and magazines. Together, with his wife, Carolyn Hunt, they have been performing storytellers known as, 'Laughing Couple', while traveling all over New England, New York, and New Jersey and performing in schools, colleges and museums. They can be seen at cultural events, powwows, and at events such as

Burlington, Vermont First Night. Laughing Couple has even had the honor of sharing a stage with the Vermont Symphony Orchestra.

CURRENTLY, Rick is working on co-curating Twisted Path III for the Abbe Museum in Bar Harbor, Maine and is also designing illustrations and paintings for various musicians projects (ie: Angie Bowie, Jeff Slate and Birds of Paradox: a band consisting of ex-members of Paul McCartney's Wings and John Lennon's Elephant Memory Band).

Rick Hunt's art is featured in private collections worldwide and can be viewed at the Abbe Museum in February, 2014.

Fancy Footwork

by

Angie Bowie

Illustrated by

Rick Hunt

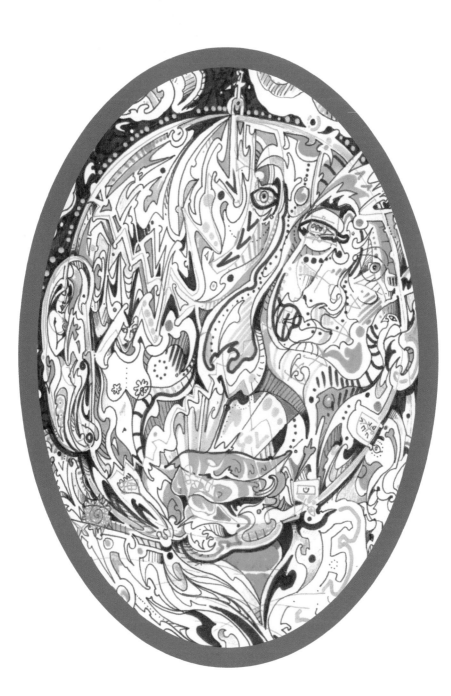

Sometimes

Sometimes when people's depth
Opens endless vistas to their beauty,
You feel a patience born of learning
You summarize the gifts, they bring to you.
Sometimes, as night closes day
It welcomes darkness
Yet it is too early to sink into dreams' repose
Then it is hard to still the thoughts
Inhabiting in your mind.
Sometimes the taste of pomegranate
Is neither kernel nor the juice,
But a surprise beneath its pulpy skin
You cannot taste or decipher,
Eating as it is, to you….
Sometimes as we ponder life,
We suck the air deep into our lungs,
And fingertips pound a beat upon the table
Pure essence is around you,
Surrounds you and it's you.
Sometimes you know the truth of death
For it is shy and at first evasive…
But experience resurrects the emotion
With such vivacity and frequency,
You know it's all that's left to you.
1974

Touch and Tell

Touch and Tell they taught, Who gives a damn?

I do and bear my heart, It's all a part...
Conditioning my soul was their only goal
Yet prophecies foretell, believing blindly leads to hell.
Who will absolve my soul?

Touch and Tell !
We tried to touch with music's love,
We tried to tell with theater's ironic dove
We sang of future and our fate but even then
We saw destruction wrought by power men...
Did you see them?

In my way I pray and also try
To heed the warnings of the fighter,
Patty Hearst, The IRA, Vietnam are not the way.
If we acknowledge light, the future will be brighter
I try to shine....

My heart's on fire to cast an ancient spell
And banish everything but peace and love to hell
I do not want the legacy I leave to old man time
Or watch original sin become his final crime
I am aware....

Light is clear, casts off disguises,

Light pierces darkness, truth surprises,

Light is gifted to a million faces.

You cannot catch or color its secret choice of places.

I will not crutch my shattered dreams and hopes

Rolling old religions up dangerous rocky slopes,

I cannot pray and thus possess

Power and Success are hateful to godliness.

1970's

Peace Party

There's a party going on,
Amongst ordinary folk,
Laughing and hoping for peace,
Peace is no joke.
Without Peace, there is no ice-cream,
Without peace, we all eat rice,
Without peace, Lovers are torn apart
Without Peace, Children are educated twice.

Life in war is high velocity,
Abbreviated time on earth,
In war an old man lives to be 30,
Middle-aged 10 year-olds ignore mirth.
Peace Party, Peace Party, Peace Party!
Party on my hands, party on my feet,
Party when I'm happy
Party when I am sweet!

So we are here; ideas guys.
Where are the old men?
Where have the professional talkers gone?
Is peace beyond their ken?
Arms dealers pickle politics,

Business corruption jettisons enthusiasm.
Working with no benefits is pay but not satisfaction.
Every country and every age has felt the spasm of war.

War is over-rated; war is messy and outdated.
One battle leads to another skirmish,
One detention questions thirty others.
The war idea is contagious and demented....
Sometimes wars are started,
Real estate won and lives lost.
Peace is the promise of the invader,
After so many wars, peace, but at what cost?

Thirty years we have hung around,
Waiting to hear of Cyprus' fate,
Thirty years we have prayed for rain,
Peace and Rain are much the same.
Where Rain falls flowers grow,
Crops feed friends, prosperity extends,
To embrace all people.

Peace is food in every town,
Peace supercharges our lives.
Peace is the ability to survive,
Peace brings leisure and high-flying dreams,
Peace is discussion, not mortal screams.

There is no country free of fear,
There is no place where the air is pure.
War beats the drum and is the soundtrack of our lives.
Peace is banished like an ugly child.
There are no ugly children,

Peace must be our mission.

2003

A Tribute to Dream Men

"We have a dream," they cried

While the sleeping woke and died

"Freedom is our dream in body and in mind.

We'll break the barriers, a new space we'll find."

Trust is progression, parallel it with passion,

Each rival rule crucifies an

important lesson.

History's recycled novelty is nature's intuition,

Adventure rampaging through time brings us to fruition!

Freedom of heart and soul

Are the only desired goal

There we can learn the trick

And speed up evolution's lazy drip

We are the outrage of expression

Physical freedom overcomes depression

Politics and war are too far removed

Your conscience only will be soothed

Total arrival is available to you

Do what you can do for what you do is you.

1976

Life's Questions....I'm just asking

Here's something that bothers me....

Why do so many people live in the past?

It is because they want to be free?

What we learn when we're young

Are the lessons we spun

To understand the world and how we fit in

Sometimes with crying, sometimes a grin.

Do all those old songs and video clips

Remind us of a time without hiccups or slips?

No, we had plenty of those

And still, we study the past.

Life in the city is different from town,

But life without convenience makes us frown.

Progress is not a dirty word

Slowing change is abusive and a little absurd.

Couldn't we wipe the slate clean?

Underneath it all we understand what we mean.

I think the desire to reserve a spot in history

Is understandable and not a mystery.

Having the tools to share every thought

Does not mean one cannot be bought.

Cherishing one's thoughts and gentling the future

Is the only passion of which I wish to be master.

Or, is it that we paddle around,

Unable to identify the different sounds

Of revolution and carnage that obviously abound?

Have we no say in the government we elect?

Or are we like ships' passengers confined to a deck?

On a spaceship that takes us to the galaxy's sights

Exploring the stars, skipping off moons and other delights?

Let's prepare for the future and behave like adults

Instead of showing our children the weak side of life

Let's enrich and embolden their futures'

With education and love, art and how to resolve strife

Let's tackle the difficult, resolve the uncool,

Bring the 21st century to every school

Our hopes and our dreams reside in the young,

Our future rides on what they become.

January 2011

Johnny

The name says it all.

You made me fall in love, into your arms.

Johnny take me for this one night

And love will be our right,

Darkness turns into light.

Johnny! Your body's soft and warm,

My senses are reborn, when will you hold me?

Johnny I touch your fingertips,

Slide my arm around your hips,

Now kiss me.

Johnny! The night will never end.

My heart needs a friend and you are he, just you baby.

Johnny. Take me for this one night,

Love will be our right,

Darkness turns into light.

Johnny! Your body's soft and warm,

My senses are reborn, when will you hold me?

Johnny! I touch your fingertips,

Slide my arm around your hips,

Now kiss me.

1987

'My interpretation of the Marlene Dietrich

original recording in German of Johnny'

Some of My Best Friends are Strangers

I've known Happiness,

And I've known sadness.

I met the Mona Lisa,

She spelt badness.

Some of my,

Some of my,

Some of my best friends are strangers.

I've known joy

And I've known sorrow,

Met a paper mache actor,

Some of my,

Some of my,

Some of my best friends are strangers.

I've had ups

I've had downs

I am acquainted with some dealers,

in a hundred towns

Some of my, Some of my,

Some of my best friends are strangers.

1975

the Sake of Fame

.or the sake of Fame,
You'll do what you have to do.
For the sake of fame,
You'll have us all do it too.
There's a time and a heart for this.
Let my soul never miss
A beat on this glorious stage of life
I made my choices and performing is my life.

Oh but for the sake of fame
I've endured some tasteless shit.
For the sake of fame
I will not continue to do it.
For the sake of fame,
You'll do what you have to do.
For the sake of fame,
You'll have us all do it too.

For the sake of fame,
I have watched people gag and choke,
For the sake of Fame,
Angst out quickly and have a stroke,
For the sake of fame,
You'll do what you have to do.
For the sake of fame,
You'll have us all do it too.

1976

Success

Success is the Bavarian Undead,

Late night places and words unsaid

Success is sitting hunched in a chair,

Pointed head and eyes that stare.

Nursing his drink, he profiles the scene.

Asking what does this all mean?

Man cannot live or love,

If he questions God above.

This is success

Go now

Success is tired,

Takes a bow

Fame bowed real low

and said real slow

Infiltrate reality

Offer it duality

He assumes a stance

In which time and success must balance.

1976

The World Is Changing

Welcome to the real world!

We're here to learn. Get far, love me

Set my life in your dreams,

By Iago's filthy schemes,

Instruments for corporate means,

The world, Yeah the world needs changing.

Face of the planet, eased by scalpel,

Is not beautified but mutillatto.

The World, Yeah the world is changing.

The Bomb.

Industry? A mistake?

Eat more.

Get fatter,

Go on a diet,

Cut down trees,

Plant alfalfa,

Cows get fatter.

Don't eat meat.

Go on a diet.

Control Heat

Air condition.

Too hot, Too cold.

Don't walk,

Jog a lot,

Get fat,

Get thin

Buy a car!

This car,

That car,

Don't walk,

Do jog.

The world, Yeah the world is changing.

Earthquakes? My mistake. People's disaster.

A Mistake? So sad. People Hurt.

Oh Earthquake. Planet getting fatter.

Earth's disaster.

Planet chunder.

Earth belch, Earth burp: Oh Planet Chunder!

Then World is Changing.

Africa between Famine and Genocide.

Apartheid is gone.

Money reality is chewed.

The burden of Mandela, Steve Biko....

Don't hurt my hero.

The World is changing.

Asia shifts and shuffles, gambles for food

Korea, China, Japan, the falling yen

Classic Stoicism – replace monarchy's upheaval.

We're here to learn. Baby it's changing.

Europe shifts from one desire to another.

Ice block thawed,

Walls torn down.

Tomorrow may be free

Doesn't mean democracy.

The world yeah the world is changing,

Honey it's changing.

American apocalypse of street fighting.

Bloods have no place to play,

NASA, The Peace Corps, stuff the war.

Explore, burn your bibles.

The world is Changing Honey it's Changing.

Girls sleeping motherhood,

Women's unrest,

Courting love on a sea of discontent.

Baby the World is Changing

America, sandwich of indecision.

Canada's calm and

The Tango passion of South America.

The double standard.

Tax drugs. Get Real

We're here to learn.

The rules are changing.

1994

God and Mr. Big

I have composed a letter
To ask a common question.
Whether to live life better
Or is it mere suggestion
That remaining puritanical
Will end in heaven's leisure
Or should we be mechanical?

Should we heed your beck and call?
Pay tithes, say prayers and go to church?
Before earth's final fall
Leaves mankind in a lurch
You are privileged and wise;
You are older than us all
Time and fate are your best mates
You've watched mighty empires fall.

I know you have a trick
That is a Chinese puzzle game.
As we tire grow old and sick
Gradually we learn it's name.

Questions asked are what you want
Your answers given are so diverse
That with philosophy you taunt
Man's quest for spiritual rebirth.

Dear You up in the sky
I have had a try;
And now methinks
It's time to quit,
Forget charades and mental skits
I love you for the care you take
When we acknowledge our mistake
Asking questions you will not answer.
They have become our intellectual cancer.
1974

Silly Satan

Silly Satan, you're a clown.
Never will you make me frown.
As you play your silly tricks.
Words and tuned play with sticks.

As you cast your fiery spells
Conjure up your tired old hells;
I can tell you plain and straight
Your promises are too late.

You pretend to make them rich
While their souls are black as pitch
You cannot win while I laugh aloud,
I will not join you, I am too proud.

I will stamp on your tail and pull off your horns,
Jump on your back and avoid your thorns.
When I am close to those I love,
I require the peace of the dove
You are banished as of now.
Out you go, kerpow!
1979

A Thought of Heaven

I have come upon a thought of heaven.

Open empty paper must promise paradise.

But why write beauty so others may admire your vision?

Is not the knowledge that you saw the truth

More blessed than the appreciation of others to this art?

An empty page holds promises of joy and ecstasy,

No written work can be superior to the promise.

It may be great and sweet and heavenly

In its inspiration but there is no assurance

That the emptiness of space

May not paint perfection more poignantly.

Words describe my thought.

Let them not be cursed for being written,

Let the idea rise above my ugly ink imprints

Let these words squeeze admiration from your heart

And satisfy my soul.

1975

For your Sweet Love…for Stacia

Verse 1:

You bring the best of times,

All the summers and sunshine.

You are the light in my heart

I cannot bear to be apart

From your sweet love

Chorus:

For your sweet love is

Why I face the day

Your sweet love is here to stay

You are all I crave and why I care

Sweet love is what we share

Verse 2:

You are the morning dew

All that shimmers and is brand new

You bring a smile to my lips

By the touch of your fingertips

Of our sweet love.

Chorus

Verse 3:

You are a doll in human form

Your sweet love is why I was born.

You are my future and my fate

I cannot make you wait

For our sweet love.

1984

Soul House

In my soul house,

There's a place

Shady rest for a daytime face.

No-one enters in that temple.

My heart alone aligns the zone.

For you are my peace,

The keeper of my eternal lease,

The lover who makes this body warm.

Now I'm standing very still,

Heart, mind and soul to accommodate.

The time for love is here.

I leave solitude

Way in the past.

Maybe I've learned at last

You are right.

I may be day,

You're surely night.

So trust in this promise I now make,

It's easy to give, far less than take.

1976

Recorded by ROY MARTIN for TRACK RECORDS

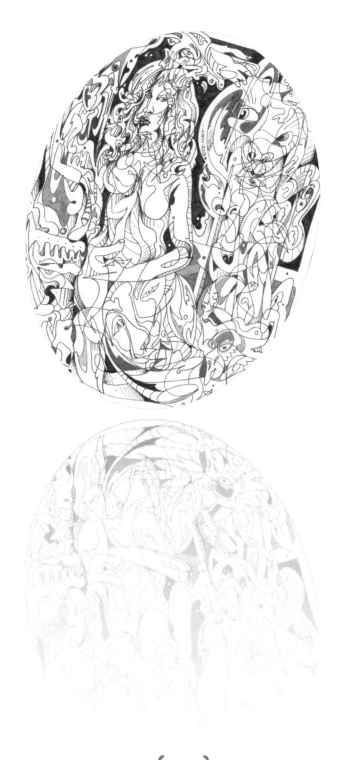

King's Cross

What a Dilemma! What a Predicament!
Someone's soldered my soul to sentiment.
Stir up the waters, I am in suspension.
Reformed, a new substance born by reflection.
What an exciting stress-filled moment,
To further confuse and confound my torment.
I crave your brain but that takes time and
And time is something "there is just too little of."

No time to play in your brain,
No time to be driven insane
Time was for collecting memories,
In a jelly jar for looking at,
under the bed at night,
with a flashlight.

No time to play in your brain,
No time to be driven insane.
Time was for collecting memories.
My memories are the written word,
Crouched under the covers, never heard,
And those words enliven me still

They are my "Enter"
My software for life.
I like your words and I like your brain
But you've already driven me insane.

I am fire and you are ice;

Got to give each other space…

Or emotions will spill onto your face.

You know how you hate that…..?

It's all about emotions and you.

1999

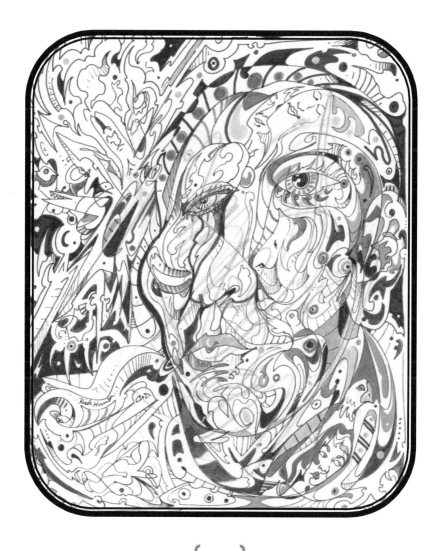

Landmarks Touched & Cherished

I am so far from landmarks touched and cherished,

An exiled lover of all that England is

A million soldiers and writers perished

To keep that land they said as 'tis.

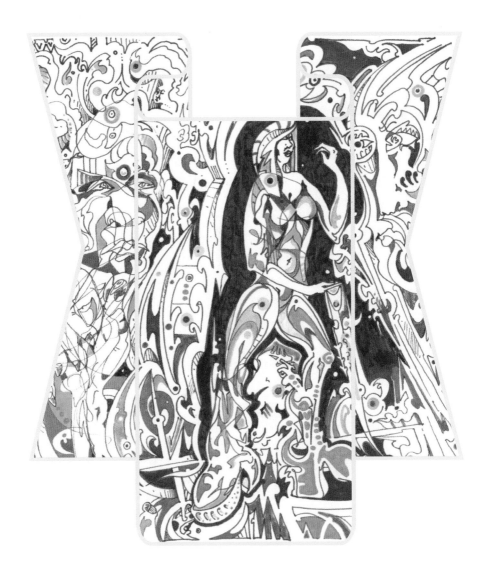

Did no-one tell our wasted youth
Tomorrow's aims are not their own.
Who warned them of the twisted truth?
Which politicians and the greedy loan
To some group called electorate,
At interest rates so high?

They risk their power every day,
People do not always buy.
How to compare a land as fair as heaven
Sweet as paradise with talent and intellect.

Electorate is surely people even as you and I.
If you now had to leave your home,
Wouldn't you rather die?
I am sad so deep inside myself,
The shock of this straight fact
Does not really connect at all.
My heart and I have made a pact.

I shall not cry for what's gone before,
I shall not swear or curse
But every day I am away from home
I shall always be the first to rave about my beautiful land
Our clever intellectuals, our brilliant industrialists
And the entertainers that entertain the world.
1975

Let's Trick Tomorrow

Let's trick tomorrow

Make it yesterday,

A sad, sweet measure

Of forgotten dreams,

Schemes long past.

Tides turned to face the future

Will be a mirror of today.

If you can turn your thoughts

Inwards and accomplish satisfaction,

Guide desires to a destined end.

When time is married

To logic's triumph,

Pleasure will be the luck of man.

Can reckless ideas govern a scheduled world?

Do laws give place to magic?

And instinct to control?

Man is motivated by one soul,

The essence of his God.

But define his God,

And you have negated instinct.

Who has the right?

I fear a time of regression

Where progress is misplaced,

Misspent and miscalculated.

Where progress is but more units of a planet's output,

Progress is the pillage and rape of her natural wealth.

The wonder that it exists at all,

Is the reason for inventing God.

1976

Time

Today, Tomorrow, Yesterday
Are Geographical Locations
In Time's Abhorrent Calendar
Where there are no Vacations

You May Stop The Video And So Rewind
Reel The Tape Back To The Beginning
Time Has No Time For These Mechanics
Youth Is Mirrored Senility Caught Grinning.

I Wonder If It's Possible
To Make Old Time A Friend
Thus Acquiring The Wisdom
We'll Need At Judgment's End.

Times Pass Methodically,
Tick Tocking Hours Of Our Lives,
Multiply The Product Of Earth Men,
And Our Energy Survives.

Future Is Projected Hopes,
The Gap In Generation,
Different From The Present,
And Vengeful Of Each Nation.

Life Is A Weary Journey,
Designed To Break Us Down,

As We Seek To Conquer,

Become Destiny's Sad Clown

Fate Is Our Memorial.

And Time And Time Again,

We Ignore The Brevity of Life,

It's Sweet Beginning And Death's End.

1977

When Family Comes to Town

Family arrives and time stands still....

A flurry of camaraderie and memory buds.

We recall our childhood and our youth.

We speak of young married days; how poor and scanty were our

possessions....

How fat and rich is the passion that cleaves us to our loved ones.

Marriages and Birthdays, Anniversaries and Celebrations,

Births and deaths, Sickness and Divorce,

Prosperity and Accomplishments,

Enthuse and fill the parachute, the fabric of our lives.

Smooth or tangled, crocheted or knitted, printed or stamped –

The end result is a thumbnail of our lives in one sweet visit.

Recall is necessary to stamp us into the flow of our time span

We enjoy the repetition amongst friendly and welcoming faces

The faces of family reward a life well-lived, by the

Adventures undertaken, hardships endured and the satisfaction of

never having missed a day of being thoroughly and fully committed to

the time and tasks required to make a living, make a family, make an

open and giving atmosphere from where to conduct our consciousness.

Focus the emotions, dismiss the ugly or negative and build on the

strength and security.

These folks are our kin. When we choose to stay we are opening up the

dam of abundance from the reservoir of love that comes from birthing

and nurturing.

There are years of steadfast loyalty, being there for counsel or support.

Thus our down days are diminished and our optimism is replenished.

We have a place to share and ignite the delight of our fellow travelers on our journey through life.

Cooking and feasting, discussing and sharing wisdom and experience
learning and enlightening the time before us. All this joy comes calling
when the family comes to town. When other conduits disappoint, our
purpose and social structure is sticky-riced to last forever by grand
architects of design who wished to bequeath us their wisdom and
experience.

What a grand event...... when families come A'calling!
This party is not over yet!
Each life is a party, a celebration of our consciousness
I had a friend who called me a drama queen; he is no longer my friend.
I had a life that was fake and humiliating, I left that life.
I had a home that was invaded by the enemy; it is no longer my home.
I had a son whom I adored; he was taught to dislike me.
He believed the lies; he is no longer on my radar.

The one thing that you can rely on life, is this....
You will be disappointed beyond belief
By those you held close, their behavior unfathomable.
You will rise above the devastating sorrow that fills your mind,
The thud of each blow as it's dealt to a prostrate body.

You will song this song: Momma, Jesus, Allah, Om mani Oh
Any God deliver me from this pain.
Then you recall, this is what sponsored the stupidity of religions –
Hopeless desperation and the cure?
It's Germanic, it's organic, it's the laughter cure.

Just whoop it up…..have a laugh,

Have a party, have a dance, do the prance,

Jockey for position and then do it all over again.

Because if not, once you're dead….it'll be Hooves Up!

Party's Over. Lights Out. The Big Sleep.

2011

Dawn is breaking…

The rain pounded all night

Suddenly the birds are chirping and gossiping

Telling stories of their dream-filled sleep adventures.

Who knew Tennessee would be so wild and wooly climate-wise?

I am impressed by the by the habitual down-pour,

Shocking day-glow blue skies follow the rain

Then It happens all over again!

Tennessee is drenched with water or sunlight

Here in the mountains there are few lights.

No cities to dazzle or brighten the sky

We are miles from anything.

As I venture to towns and cities,

There are no crowds.

Folks talk softly and seem surprised

By the sound of laughing out loud....

The Smoky mountains surround us and we are suspended in time

Only the cutting and mowing holds back Mother Nature

People are a footnote to the lay of the land

There is no arguing with the tempo it demands....

Hold my hand, let's walk a while

Climb a hill and hike a mile

Now the fog is clinging to the trees

I love the birdsong as they rev up for a new day,

Hold my hand and here we'll stay.

2014

Far From Me Tonight

Tu es trop loin de moi ce soir,
Mon Coeur mange ton desespoir,
Et pour que je ne me reveille pas en peur,
J'espere que tu te moques pas de moi

Oh You are too far from me tonight,
Oh my heart eats up your despair
Lest I wake crying in fright,
I pray that you don't care.

You are too like a soul I knew,
Someone now best forgot
Whose falsehoods sounded oh so true
In the time that time forgot.

Tu es trop loin de moi ce soir
Mon Coeur mange ton desespoir,
Et pour que je ne me reveille pas en peur,
J'espere que tu te moques pas de moi
Oh You are too far from me tonight,
Oh my heart eats up your despair
Lest I wake crying in fright,

I pray that you don't care.

And if it's fear I ask myself,
Why did we start again?
Did you think you'd make me cry?
Did you think I'd scream and sigh…

Oh no, You are too far from me tonight,
Oh my heart eats up your despair
Lest I wake crying in fright,
I pray that you don't care.

Now it's time to test my resolution
 and see if I am lacking,
Now it's time to tap the mask
 and see if I am cracking.

Tu es trop loin de moi ce soir,
Mon Coeur mange ton desespoir,
Et pour que je ne me reveille pas en peur,
J'espere que tu te moques pas de moi

Oh You are too far from me tonight,
Oh my heart eats up your despair
Lest I wake crying in fright,
I pray that you don't care.

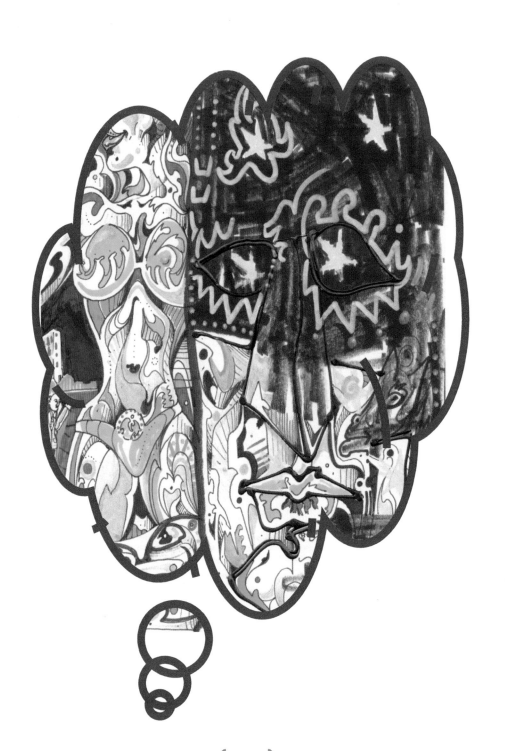

Take Out Your Troubles

Take out your troubles,

Wrap them in a bag,

Take out your worries and throw them outside

If your troubles are too many

Why not get a bigger case?

Close the lid lock it down.

 Lay them, in a final resting place.

When your smile is pasted on,

You can drive the care downtown

When your date is two hours late,

Tell them to rendezvous with fate,

When your hat blows in the wind,

Your dress whips up and your hair is pinned

Kick off your shoes and run in bare feet

You'll be fine running down the street.

Cool your fins. Blow your jets.

Shark's delight.

Brain's on fire.

You'll be there all night.

Take out your heart,

Give it a shake,

Rub out the dust,

Make a cake,

Bake your love a new set of rules,

Stay with me, I won't be fooled

 if you cheat or tell a lie

 you'll be gone before the sun hits the sky

You'll be thrown out in the street

 Shoes, keys, pants and beer, all at your feet.

Cool your fins. Blow your jets.

Shark's delight.

Brain's on fire.

You'll be there all night.

Take out your troubles,

Wrap them in a bag,

Take out your worries and throw them outside.

If your troubles are too many

Why not get a bigger case?

Close the lid lock it down.

Lay them, in a final resting place.

Cool your fins.

Blow your jets.

Shark's delight.

Brain's on fire.

You'll be there all night.

2012

Lyrics – Angela Bowie Barnett

Music – Chico Rey and Charlie Rey

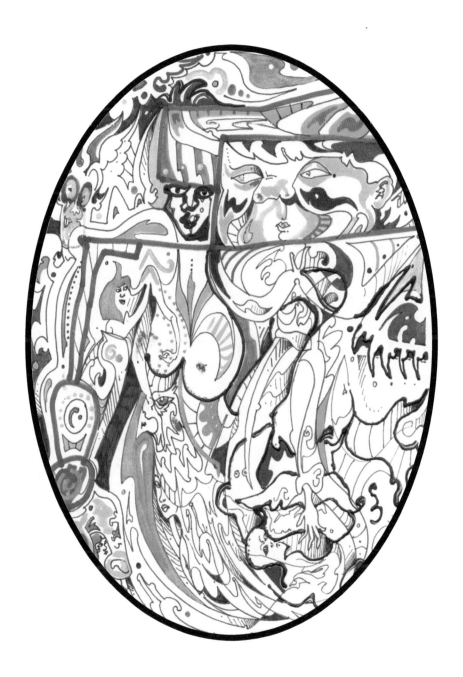

Danse, Danse, Danse

Danse, Danse, Danse,

Danse The night away,

Danse, Danse, Danse

Danse The night away

You're my heart's desire

Make it your heart, too…..

Kiss my heart, you're a part

Part of my desire

Danse, Danse, Danse.

Danse the night away

Danse, Danse, Danse

Danse The night away

You Live long and sweet

Danse me off my feet,

If I love, if your face is

going to be the love

Kiss, Kiss, Kiss

Mwah mwah

Oo Po ppa. Oo Pa pa

Oh papapapapapapapapa

Oh Yeah I'll take a drink

Kiss me

Danse Danse Danse

Danse the night away

Oooooooo

 Danse Danse Danse

Danse the night away

Danse, Danse, Danse

Oh whatever you say big Boy

Ooooo owowowwow

Danse

 Wow wowowoww

Kiss me Kiss kiss kiss

Danse Danse Danse

Kiss me

Kiss Kiss Kiss Kiss Kiss Kiss Kiss me

Kiss

2009

Lyrics – Angela Bowie Barnett

Music – Chic Cashman

Fires Are Burning

Fires are burning in the forests of youth.

Rebels are spurning their moments of truth.

God he is laughing upstairs all alone.

You, you are burning as we gently moan.

Times they are changing, for girls and for boys,

Reality replacing idle dreams for toys.

My fire is burning especially for you.

My heart is spurning the lies they tell about you

Keep on burning fire....

Fires are burning in the forest of youth,

Rebels are spurning their motives of truth.

You and I are laughing upstairs all alone

We're gently burning all our barriers down.

1975

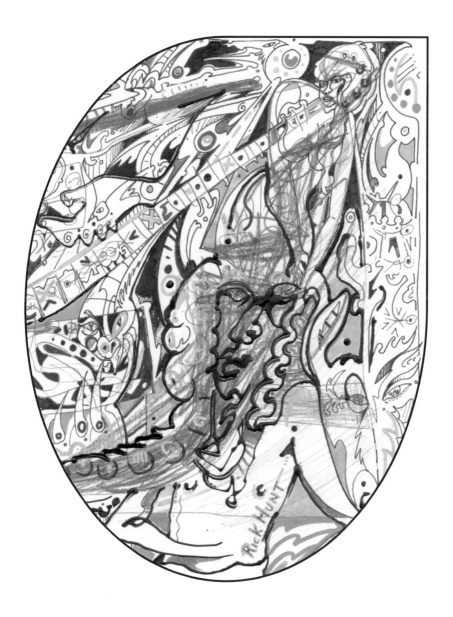

Romeo of Romance

You are my Romeo of Romance,

Love you, a vision entranced

You are all I crave to be

You're with my soul for eternity...

And I know that you speak without words,

And I know that you speak without words

Because you speak without words

Your smile and shining eyes,

Do not really surprise me.

Your laugh and great big strength,

Are how a man is supposed to be,

And I know that you speak without words

And I know that you speak without words

And a love that's true speaks without words

And a love that's true speaks without words

Because you speak without words

Because you speak without words

Instrumental

You are my Juliet of Romance,

Without you I am in a trance.

You are life's mystery,

Only your touch will set me free

And I know that you speak without words

1986

From the album MOON GODDESS

Seeking to get Closer to Heaven

Feel your touch of magic,

Let me feel a body strong,

If I sing of virtue fallen,

Will you pardon all that's wrong?

My gift is your wisdom,

If I'm worthy of your time,

Let me know,

Will you bring me closer to heaven?

As our today is your tomorrow.

Bring me closer to heaven, Closer than my song,

Heaven's close as the day is long

Bring me closer to heaven,

Bring me closer to my soul,

Closer to heaven,

Bring me closer to my soul

I will light the night with fire,

Star shine your rocky way,

Give you all I know

That's all my songs can say

So bring me closer to heaven,

Bring me closer to my song,

Closer to heaven

Bring me closer to heaven,

Closer than my song,

Heaven's close as the day is long

Bring me closer to heaven,

Closer than my soul.

1979

Suicide Mocked

Down days are companions
To suicides recurring gloom.
Despair re-opens iron gates
To a forgotten and lonely tomb.
I reach and try to touch
My evasive friend the sun,
A symbol of ecstasy
And long-lost childhood fun.
Life stretches futurely
And points to the unknown.
But the bird of paradise
Has already flown.

Sentiment and passion have been pushed aside
The fall of virtue is Karma, brutally denied.
Guilt, the mind's religious confession
Teaches us one important lesson.
Man craves cruel perfection and astonishing good
His energy and manners dictate just how he should.

I am the anguished talent of lost and faded dreams
Sacrificed to fulfill another's grandiose world schemes
Night beckons me with her chaotic screams.
I comply for terror causes blood to boil
Let me soon return to her
The welcoming arms of Earth's fertile soil
1976

My heart is heavy…

My heart is heavy, my eyes are full of tears,

The solution evades me as I hide from my fears.

Fear of poverty, death, homelessness and poor health.

Poverty is known to me,

My brain manufactured all my wealth,

Death is inevitable, another road ending before our eyes.

I am not ready, I want to refute the power mongers' lies,

That are piloting the spaceship Earth.

It will come unleashed and never reach,

The planet for man's rebirth.

We cannot always effect the changes,

We know should come.

We rebuild the hazy life,

We have become.

Sadness overwhelms my soul,

I am lost thrashing near the final goal.

But I stay entranced, watching lives whirl past

Wondering which birth,

Which meal,

Which war,

Which smile …….. will be my last?

2012

My Heart Beats faster

When the candles flicker
My heart beats faster
Distress and anguish flood my soul
I cling to my mirrored face
As I search the structure and windows
 that house my thoughts,
I feel reassurance.
I examine every inch to ensure I am still real.
Does this happen to you too?

Feel my heart beat faster, each line I take,
makes me want to live louder
How can I tattoo my pulse
So I may flourish and draw the dreams
But love, feel my heart beat faster, faster.
I'm thrilling to my high,
I be and am and reach for the sky.
The love you shoot me with a look
Is the anchor of knowledge we discover in books.
What thirsty children for truth we are
Will this new experience take us far?
Will we learn the solutions we have sought
Or is this the battle inquiring minds have always fought?
Feel our hearts beat faster gentle friend.
We are capturing soul force, making it send
A thousand answers for the soothing of this

Speeding heart, gently love you're slowing down
You've lived the moment, gone the frown,
Now feel my heart as it slows and slows
The answers come reeling, heart and mind come to blows
Slow down heart, we've tried this high
Every question we shall gradually untie.
Now my heart beats in time again.
1975

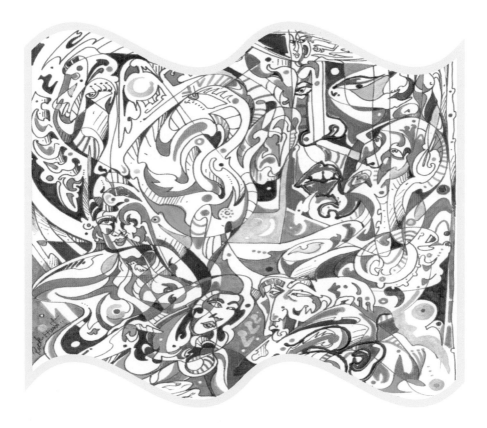

Come Visit My Erotic Fantasy

Come, visit my erotic fantasy
Make it your reality.
Loosen the chains binding you to life,
Strip off frustration with scalpel and knife.

We gave you a knife called intellect,
You buy your freedom, send it collect.
The scalpel is conditioning,
Mutilates your soul.
Instincts are cracked
Like clouds with rainy holes.
Postage is paid by parents' guilty tears.
A fuck is birth sponsored by women's fears.

Come, entertain my morning dream,
Quieten my shuddering scream.
The pleasures polished in your mind
Are really freedom, that which makes you kind.

Without the closeness of another's breath,
Without the touch of someone's flesh,
Without the kiss of talking lips,
Without the thrust of narrow hips,
Without a cock stretching towards my heart,
Without your love I fall apart.

Come, is all you need,

Come and smile, Come Indeed.

Come in your love and for all others,

Start with coming and men will be brothers.

1976

I wrote this as lyrics for a musical (in development) with Lionel Bart,
Jean Genet and produced by Kit Lambert and Chris Stamp of Track
Records. The show was never staged. And we had the same censorship
problems when we staged and wrote the Los Angeles version Of Krisis
Kabaret.

Soul Sad

I feel your presence, like a pleasure dream,
My heart's on fire, my brain could scream.
There is no joy in silent anguish, only a bequest
Sent to you as a tribute of your conquest.

She knew you well, her heart was won
When Love reached out and made you one.
The puppets who danced at her command
Would never satisfy the girl's demand.

No hard, hip artist, to live in separation,
Was the joy she sought or her dream sensation.
No rich indulgent fleeting coupling
Or fame increased by Star-fuckers' suckling.

No pretty boy she could make so rich
And as time marched on make him her bitch.
No, for you there had to be a desperate soul,
Ripe for the cunning fairytale you told

He alone planned with care
To force this love to share.
He achieved this act sublime
And counted it on the clocks of time.
He executed his plan with patience long
By flattery and being strong

Is capture of a rare bird cruel?

If you'd dreamed your life as glamour's fool

There is no orgasm for beauty's queen

Fame buys envy and all things mean

He stole your heart and as you looked around,

Body, soul and face were never to be found.

1977

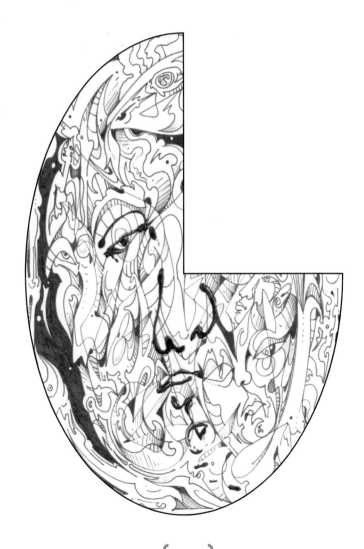

Made in the USA
Charleston, SC
14 May 2015